Little Leaders
From Heaven

KISA KIDS PUBLICATIONS
Under the Guidance of Moulana Nabi R. Mir (Abidi)

Preface

Prophet Muḥammad (s): Nurture and raise your children in the best way. Raise them with the love of the Prophets and the Ahlul Bayt (a).

Literature is an influential form of media that often shapes the thoughts and views of an entire generation. Therefore, in order to establish an Islamic foundation for the future generations, there is a dire need for compelling Islamic literature. Over the past several years, this need has become increasingly prevalent throughout Islamic centers and schools everywhere. Due to the growing dissonance between parents, children, society, and the teachings of Islām and the Ahlul Bayt (a), this need has become even more pressing. Al-Kisa Foundation, along with its subsidiary, Kisa Kids Publications, was conceived in an effort to help bridge this gap with the guidance of ʿulamah and the help of educators. We would like to make this a communal effort and platform. Therefore, we sincerely welcome constructive feedback and help in any capacity.

Little Leaders From Heaven takes you back to the childhood days of our beloved Imam Hasan (a) and Imam Husain (a) with five engaging stories.The goal of this book is to help children form a lasting connection with two of the best role models, the leaders of the youth of paradise, Imam Hasan (a) and Imam Husain (a). Through inspiring stories that exemplify their status, wisdom, purity, kindness and compassion, your children will take away important lessons that they can apply in their own lives.

With Du'ās,
Nabi R. Mir (Abidi)

Disclaimer: Religious texts have ***not*** been translated verbatim so as to meet the developmental and comprehension needs of children.

Dedication

This book is dedicated to the beloved Imām of our time (AJ). May Allāh (swt) hasten his reappearance and help us to become his true companions.

Acknowledgments

Prophet Muḥammad (s): The pen of a writer is mightier than the blood of a martyr.

True reward lies with Allāh, but we would like to sincerely thank Sisters Sabika Mithani, Fatemah Meghji, Fatemah Mithani-Hussain, Irum Abbas, Marwa Kachmar, Farwa Nawab, Zahra Sabur, Farheen Abbas and Fatima Hussain. May Allāh bless them in this world and the next.

Please recite a Fātiḥa for
the marḥūmīn of the Mithani, Hussain,
Nawab family, and Syed Yusuf Hasan

Contents

Chapter 1
The Little Teachers

Splash!

Imam Hasan (a) blinked twice as a fist full of water splattered all over him!

With a playful grin, Imam Husain (a) looked at his big brother, who was now completely soaked and dripping with water.

The day was hot, and the two brothers were playing near a small, quaint, pond on the outskirts of Medina. Medina is the city of their grandfather, the Prophet (s) of Allah. They enjoyed playing outdoors, as they could see the wonders of Allah's creation, and reflect on the signs of Allah's *Jamaal*, His *beauty*.

As the sun became bright, an elderly man made his way toward the tiny pond where the two brothers were playing. The time of prayer was approaching, and the man wanted to perform wudhu so that he could join the Prophet (s) at the masjid for salaah. The man knelt down and splashed his face with water, delighted at how refreshing it felt. He thanked Allah for providing such cooling water on this intensely hot day.

The two young Imams (a) saw the man from a
distance and recognized him as he would often pray
behind their grandfather at the masjid.

The Imams (a) made their way toward the pond to greet the elderly man.

"Salaamun alaikum Uncle!" the brothers politely said. The Imams (a) called him 'uncle' out of love and respect.

The elderly man looked up lovingly at the two young grandsons of the Prophet (s) of Allah.

He could not help but smile happily at the two bright faces staring back at him!

"Wa alaikum salaam my dear boys," he replied.

The man looked back down toward the water and started carefully performing his wudhu with focus, but, oh no! He made a mistake!

Imam Hasan (a) and Imam Husain (a) wanted what was best for others, so they dearly wanted the elderly man to perform his wudhu correctly.

But how could the Imams (a) correct him without embarrassing or upsetting him? Well, the young Imams (a) always did everything in the best of ways, and just then, like a lightbulb, they came up with the perfect plan!

The two young Imams (a) knelt down by the pond and began to chat, just loud enough for the elderly man to hear them.

"I do my wudhu perfectly!" said Imam Hasan (a) to his brother.

"Umm... I think mine is better!" replied Imam Husain (a).

"I don't think so! Oh, I have an idea! Maybe we should ask the uncle who can do wudhu better?" said Imam Hasan (a).

So, he turned to the elderly man and asked him, "Dear Uncle! Can you help us by judging to see who performs wudhu in the most perfect way?"

"Of course! I will certainly try to help," replied the elderly man, smiling.

The plan was working!

The elderly man watched as the young Imams (a) took turns performing their wudhu. He watched as they performed their wudhu with extreme care and love, and *exactly* in the same way!

Oh my! He immediately realized that it was actually *his* wudhu that was incorrect!

After the two Imams (a) finished, Imam Hasan (a) asked, "Dear Uncle, which one of us did our wudhu the best?"

The man looked at the Imams (a) with tears in his eyes. He couldn't believe how kind and pure these two young boys were in how they showed him his mistakes!

"Both of you did your wudhu with absolute perfection! I have been the one performing *my* wudhu with mistakes. I thank Allah for showing me my errors, and I ask forgiveness from Allah, the Almighty! I am so thankful that He chose the pure grandsons of the Prophet (s) to teach me in such a beautiful manner!"

And with those words, the man performed his wudhu once more. This time, he did it in the correct way just as he had learned!

Chapter 2
Intercessors

"One...
two...
three...

JUMP!"

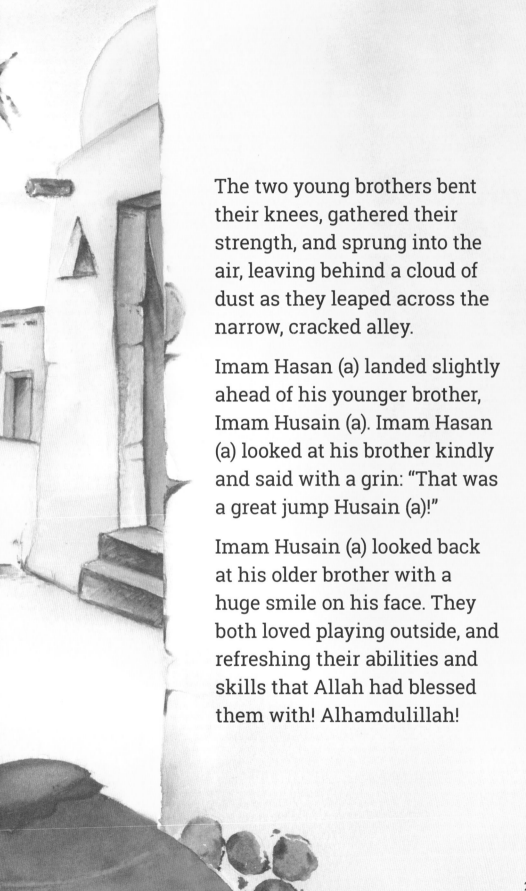

The two young brothers bent their knees, gathered their strength, and sprung into the air, leaving behind a cloud of dust as they leaped across the narrow, cracked alley.

Imam Hasan (a) landed slightly ahead of his younger brother, Imam Husain (a). Imam Hasan (a) looked at his brother kindly and said with a grin: "That was a great jump Husain (a)!"

Imam Husain (a) looked back at his older brother with a huge smile on his face. They both loved playing outside, and refreshing their abilities and skills that Allah had blessed them with! Alhamdulillah!

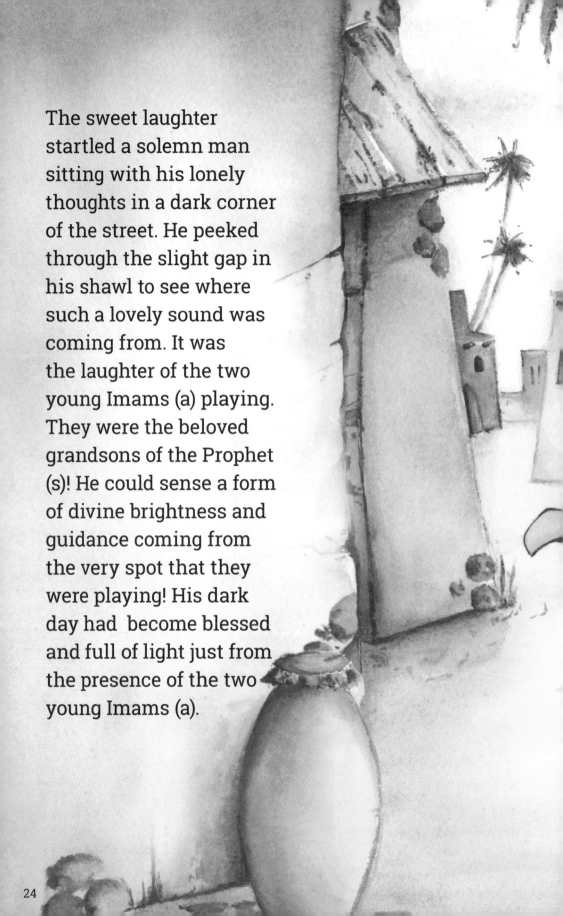

The sweet laughter startled a solemn man sitting with his lonely thoughts in a dark corner of the street. He peeked through the slight gap in his shawl to see where such a lovely sound was coming from. It was the laughter of the two young Imams (a) playing. They were the beloved grandsons of the Prophet (s)! He could sense a form of divine brightness and guidance coming from the very spot that they were playing! His dark day had become blessed and full of light just from the presence of the two young Imams (a).

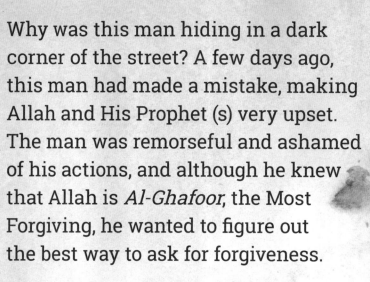

Why was this man hiding in a dark corner of the street? A few days ago, this man had made a mistake, making Allah and His Prophet (s) very upset. The man was remorseful and ashamed of his actions, and although he knew that Allah is *Al-Ghafoor*, the Most Forgiving, he wanted to figure out the best way to ask for forgiveness.

The man was too ashamed to see his friends, to enter the masjid, and especially to see the Prophet (s) of Allah. He wandered the streets of Medina lost in thought for days, but could not figure out the best way to ask for forgiveness. It was only when he saw the two young Imams (a) playing that his dark thoughts brightened and a brilliant plan began to form in his mind!

With hope, the man began walking toward the grandsons of the Prophet (s).

The two brothers paused their game when they noticed a man walking toward them. The man kept his face down, avoiding eye contact with the young Imams (a).

"Salaamun alaikum, O children of Rasulullah (s)," he said in a low voice as he reached the spot where the two young Imams (a) were standing.

The brothers recognized the sad man! He lived nearby and often prayed at the masjid, and sat with their grandfather. The Imams (a) could see the deep sadness in the man's eyes. They responded warmly to his greeting, saying "Wa alaikum salaam dear Uncle." The two Imams (a) were so welcoming and sincere that the man could not help but smile.

The man looked at the bright faces in front of him and understood why the Prophet (s) of Allah loved these two Imams (a) so dearly.

With a heart full of hope, the man took a deep breath, praying that his plan would work.

The man wanted to carry the two Imams (a) on his shoulders just as he had seen the Prophet (s) of Allah do before. He asked the Imams (a), and when they happily agreed, he swooped them up onto his shoulders and started briskly walking through the busy streets of Medina, making his way toward the masjid, eagerly wanting to talk to the Prophet (s) of Allah.

The man's heart was pounding and full of hope as he approached the masjid. The moment that he could be forgiven was now here! He took a deep breath and made his way to Rasulullah (s) who was busy talking to his companions.

The man entered the courtyard of the masjid with
the two Imams (a) still on his shoulders. He knew
that Allah and His Prophet (s) loved these two young
Imams (a) dearly. He was hoping that this love would
act as a bridge to help him gain Allah's forgiveness.

With his head bent down, the man slowly began to approach the Prophet (s) with tears in his eyes, "Salaamun alaikum, O Rasulullah (s), I am very sorry for my bad actions and I ask Allah, the Almighty, for forgiveness. On my shoulders, I have two shining stars, your pure grandsons!"

The man continued to look down and did not hear a sound. He began to worry, but then heard a sweet chuckle.

When he looked up, to his surprise he saw the Prophet (s) grinning from ear to ear, looking at him with love and respect. "Wa alaikum salaam! Surely this is a great idea!" said Rasulullah (s). The Prophet (s) loved his two grandsons very much because Allah loved them so dearly. This man was trying to use this love to help him seek forgiveness. Clearly, he regretted the mistakes he had made, and was trying his best to fix them! With a smile on his face, the Prophet (s) told him, "Don't worry! Allah has forgiven you and cleansed you of your mistakes!"

The man fell to the floor in sajdah with tears of joy in his eyes, and thanked Allah for this blessing of forgiveness. He kissed the Prophet's (s) hands with happiness. Now that he knew he had been forgiven, he felt so free!

The Prophet (s) of Allah admiringly gazed at his dear grandsons with affection and said, "O leaders of the youth of paradise! You have done *shifa'ah*, which means intercession, for this man and Allah has accepted this man's apology because of His love for you!"

Manāqib Āal Abī Ṭālib, Vol. 3, Pg. 400

Chapter 3
The Little Champions

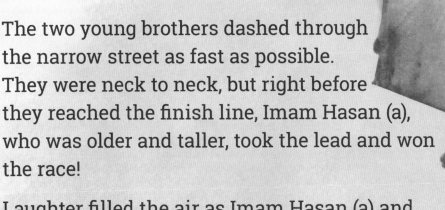

The two young brothers dashed through the narrow street as fast as possible. They were neck to neck, but right before they reached the finish line, Imam Hasan (a), who was older and taller, took the lead and won the race!

Laughter filled the air as Imam Hasan (a) and Imam Husain (a) tried to catch their breaths. The brothers loved to play with each other and challenge one another in activities like racing, jumping, and even wrestling! They knew that their physical abilities were a blessing from Allah the Almighty and would continuously thank Him throughout their play.

As they were busy playing, their beloved grandfather, Allah's final Messenger (s), walked toward them. The sound of their playful laughter warmed his heart and put a divine smile on his face. He loved his grandsons because Allah loved them.

Imam Husain (a) looked up and saw his grandfather coming. He left his game and ran into his arms for a massive hug. Imam Hasan (a) did the same thing and both brothers cried out together in unison: "Salaamun alaikum dear grandfather!"

"Wa alaikum salaam my dear grandsons! What have you been playing this morning?" The two young Imams (a) eagerly told their grandfather about the various activities and games they had been playing. The Prophet (s) then picked them up and placed them on his shoulders as he often did. Together, they began heading toward the home of Sayyidah Fatimah (a).

As they approached the house, Imam Hasan (a) and Imam Husain (a) climbed down from the shoulders of the Prophet (s) and ran toward the house to greet and hug their mother. "Salaamun alaikum! Mother, Mother! Look who is here!" Sayyidah Fatimah (a) smiled at her sons and smothered them with kisses, and responded by saying "Wa alaikum salaam the lights of my eyes!" She then looked up and saw that her beloved father was coming through the door. Her face lit up as she greeted him with a warm hug, and said "Saalamun alaikum beloved father!"

After they ate a small snack, the two brothers went outside. Imam Hasan (a) looked at his younger brother with a smile and said, "Husain (a), want to have a wrestling match?"

Imam Husain (a) looked at his brother with a grin, and nodded. He loved it when they played different sports that challenged them.

As they began the match, their grandfather and mother came outside to watch them. This made the two young brothers even more excited!

Prophet Muhammad (s) watched the two boys challenge each other. "MashaAllah, excellent move, Hasan (a)! Quick! Grab Husain (a)!" he cheered as he watched.

Sayyidah Fatimah (a) curiously looked at her father and asked, "O father, why are you only cheering for Hasan (a) when he is older and stronger? What about Husain (a)?" She knew that her father was always fair and must have had a good reason.

Rasulullah (s) smiled wisely, looked at his daughter, and said, "O my beloved daughter, don't worry about Husain (a). There is someone very special who is cheering for him!"

Sayyidah Fatimah (a) looked at her father all puzzled and asked, "Who is cheering him on, dear father?"

"The high angel of the heavens is! The same one who reveals the verses of the Quran to me, none other than Angel Jibraeel! These two boys are loved by the angels because they are not only leaders who will guide people in this world, but will be the leaders of paradise as well!"

Sayyidah Fatimah's (a) face glowed with honor! She thanked Allah for these two little heavenly leaders, and continued to watch her sons play.

Imam Hasan (a), knowing that he was older and stronger, very lovingly decided to let his brother pin him down and win the match.

The sun had now reached its brightest point and the time for Dhuhr salaah had approached. The two young Imams (a) climbed back onto the shoulders of the Prophet (s) of Allah, and happily headed toward the masjid, delighted to remember and thank Allah for their blessed day through prayer. Alhamdulillah!

Sheikh Mufīd, Al-Irshād, Vol.2 Pg.128

Chapter 4
Leaders of Paradise

"Tag!"

Imam Hasan (a) tapped his younger brother's shoulder and raced down the empty streets of Medina. The hot sun was blazing down on the quiet city as the people were in their homes resting after the afternoon prayers.

"Don't worry I'll catch you this time!" called out Imam Husain (a) as he ran as fast as he could.

With Imam Hasan (a) in the lead, the two brothers sped through the streets toward the outskirts of the city, heading to the pond.

Imam Hasan (a) slowed down, giving his brother a chance to catch up. Imam Husain (a) quickly caught up and triumphantly tackled his brother out of excitement.

"Husain (a), you won! MashaAllah!" Imam Hasan (a) exclaimed witha smile on his face. He hugged him and quietly thanked Allah for blessing him with such an amazing younger brother.

It was midday and the scorching afternoon sun blazed down on the Imams (a). After so much running, the brothers needed to rest and re-energize. They washed their faces and drank water from the cool pond. Imam Hasan (a) looked at his younger brother and said, "Doesn't this water feel amazing on such a hot day, Husain (a)? Alhamdulillah!" The young Imams (a) were always thankful to Allah the Almighty for providing them with exactly what they needed. They knew that above all, Allah was *Ar-Raziq*, the Provider.

The brothers were exhausted and decided to rest. As they lay down, they gazed at the beautiful bright sky above them. Slowly, their eyes began to close and before they knew it, they were fast asleep under the shade of a palm tree.

Back in the city, near the masjid, the smell of freshly baked bread lingered out from the home of Sayyidah Fatimah (a). She was busy preparing lunch for her beloved sons whom she knew would be hungry and tired when they returned home.

As Sayyidah Fatimah (a) finished baking, Umm Aimen, her dear friend and helper, went outside to call the two brothers inside for lunch. Umm Aimen soon came back inside, but without the two Imams (a)!

"Umm Aimen, you're alone! Where are the boys?" asked Sayyidah Fatimah (a).

"I'm not sure! I couldn't find them nearby," Umm Aimen replied.

"I'm sure they will be home shortly, inshaAllah. They're always careful to return home on time," said Sayyidah Fatimah (a).

After some time had passed, and the two Imams (a) had not yet returned, Sayiddah Fatimah (a) whispered a dua to Allah, asking Him for their safe return. She looked at her friend and said, "I'm a little concerned Umm Aimen... the boys are never late, and it's a very hot day today. Perhaps they stopped somewhere to rest. I should ask my father for advice. Maybe he knows where they have gone!"

Umm Aimen looked at the Lady of Light, her most beloved friend, and said, "Let me go and ask the Prophet (s) of Allah for you, O Fatimah az-Zahra (a)!"

Sayiddah Fatimah (a) smiled and agreed, noticing how eager Umm Aimen was to help. Umm Aimen quickly got ready and set off to meet Rasulullah (s).

Umm Aimen found the Prophet (s) of Allah with his companions near the masjid. She hurried over to him and said, "Salaamun alaikum, O Rasulullah (s)! Your grandsons went out to play, but haven't returned home for lunch. Do you happen to know where they are?"

Prophet Muhammad (s) responded, "Wa alaikum salaam Umm Aimen. Hmm... it is very much unlike them to be late, especially if they know their mother is expecting them.
InshaAllah, everything is okay." The Prophet (s) raised his hands in prayer and made a dua to Allah, "Ya Rabbi! O my Lord! Please keep Hasan (a) and Husain (a) safe and always keep them under Your protection and care."

As soon as he finished the dua, the Prophet's (s) face changed color as it usually did when he would receive a *wahi*, or revelation from Allah. After a few moments, the Prophet (s) broke into a smile.

He turned to Umm Aimen and said, "Tell my beloved daughter not to worry. I will bring them home! Angel Jibraeel just came to me and said, 'Salaam and blessings upon you O Rasulullah (s). Your two grandsons are a divine creation of Allah. They are protected with a heavenly protection. They have a great status not only in this world, but also in the hereafter, as they are the leaders of the youth of paradise!'"

Soon after, the Prophet (s) arrived at the pond and found his grandsons soundly sleeping under a palm tree. Behind them stood a magnificent angel guarding and protecting these two leaders from heaven.

SubhanAllah! These two young Imams (a) were certainly divinely protected! They were the chosen leaders of Allah, chosen to guide everyone to the right path. Prophet Muhammad (s) loved his grandsons immensely as they were loved by Allah! He knelt down, and gently gave them both a kiss on their foreheads, waking them softly.

The brothers stirred awake and saw the shining face of their grandfather gazing down on them. They jumped up, and playfully tackled their grandfather, giving him a huge hug. Rasulullah (s) lifted Imam Hasan (a) and Imam Husain (a) onto his shoulders and started walking toward Sayyidah Fatimah's (a) home where he knew she was eagerly waiting to see them.

As they were walking home, Imam Ali (a) saw them and immediately thanked Allah that his two sons were safe. Imam Ali (a) greeted the Prophet (s) and his sons with a salaam, and said, "Alhamdulillah, I'm glad to see that both of you are not only okay, but are also getting to ride on the best of shoulders!" Imam Hasan (a) and Imam Husain (a) smiled at their father. Prophet Muhammad (s) looked at his cousin and said, "O Ali (a), I'm the one who is blessed as I have the best riders on my shoulders!"

As they all arrived home, Sayyidah Fatimah (a) greeted her two sons with hugs and kisses. She was so happy and relieved to have them home! She thanked Allah for honoring them with His protection. Sayyidah Fatimah (a) served the fresh bread she had baked with some yogurt. The beloved Ahlul Bayt (a), Sayyidah Fatimah (a), her father, her husband, and her two sons, then sat together to share their tasty and blessed lunch!

Chapter 5
Heavenly Gift

"Hasan (a)! Get ready! Incoming!" called out Imam Husain (a) as he kicked the ball toward his older brother. Imam Hasan (a) caught the ball swiftly with his feet, carefully dribbling it as he darted past the opposing team, picking up speed until he caught sight of Abdullah.

He looked left, right, and left
again before passing the ball to
Abdullah, who aimed between the two
trees and kicked as hard as he could.
Another player tried to snatch the
ball, but failed. It went past him, beyond
the trees and...**SCORE!** Imam Husain (a)
and Imam Hasan (a) cheered! Their team had won
the game!

Laughter filled the air as the boys cheered,
grinning from ear to ear. However, this was not the
only reason the two brothers and their friends were
excited. It was the day before Eid, and the streets
were buzzing with energy as the people of Medina
prepared for the festivities.

The bazaar was crowded with various vendors, who were selling clothes, jewelry, fruits, and of course, freshly baked sweets!

The two brothers sat below a palm tree to rest after their amazing game. As they observed the buzz of the bazaar, their good friend, Abdullah, joined them.

"Abdullah, that was a great kick! You played well today, MashaAllah!" Imam Hasan (a) exclaimed. He scooted over to make some space for his friend to sit next to them.

"Alhamdulillah! And you made a great pass at the perfect time to make the winning score!" Abdullah responded with a big grin.

"Oh, I should go! There's my mother! She had said to meet her at the bazaar. She wants to take me to a tailor

to take measurements for my new outfit for Eid tomorrow! InshaAllah I will see you both at the masjid for Eid prayers!" Abdullah got up and ran to meet his mother.

As Imam Husain (a) watched Abdullah run over to his mother, he turned to his brother and asked, "Hasan (a), what are we wearing for Eid tomorrow?" Imam Hasan (a) looked at his brother and said with a smile, "I'm not sure, but why don't we go home and ask Mama?"

The young Imams (a) started walking toward their
home, the noise of the bazaar fading behind them.

Sayyidah Fatimah (a) was busy preparing for the
last iftaar of the month of Ramadhan when her sons
arrived home.

"Salaamun alaikum Mama!" they said as they ran up to her, kissing her hand and greeting her with a hug.

"Wa alaikum salaam my dear boys! How was your game?" Sayyidah Fatimah (a) asked.

"It was great! Hasan (a) made an amazing pass to Abdullah, who scored the winning goal!" Imam Husain (a) responded enthusiastically.

"MashaAllah that's great! Seems like you enjoyed yourselves, alhamdulillah!" Sayyidah Fatimah (a) said with a smile.

"Mama, do you need help preparing iftaar?" asked Imam Hasan (a). "No, thank you! You both must be tired. Why don't you two rest for a bit?" She gave them both a kiss on their foreheads.

As the two brothers were leaving, Imam Husain (a) paused and asked his mother, "Mama if tomorrow is Eid, will we be wearing new clothes?"

Sayyidah Fatimah (a) looked at her beloved sons with a smile and said, "Let me talk to your father and see what we can do."

Sayyidah Fatimah (a) knew it would be difficult to get new clothes made for Eid as their finances were a bit tight. Regardless, she would make dua and try her best. She knew that if she placed her trust in Allah, He would ensure the best of results.

Imam Ali (a) arrived home as the two brothers were still soundly asleep. Sayyidah Fatimah (a) asked him about the Eid clothes. Imam Ali (a) wasn't sure but said he would try his best.

The brothers awoke with the sound of their father's voice. They rushed to give their salaams to him. Imam Ali (a) looked at his two sons and said, "This may be the last few moments before this great month of Allah comes to an end. If tomorrow is the day of Eid, that is the day Allah will reward us with the good deeds we have earned during this month inshaAllah."

"May Allah accept our deeds! Be sure to do some extra special prayers tonight as it is a very special night!" said Sayyidah Fatimah (a) to her sons.
"Also, remember we will start off the day tomorrow with the Eid ghusl. As we wash our bodies we should pray to Allah to clean our souls as well.

We will then join our family, friends, and fellow believers at the masjid for Eid prayers. I'm sure there will be many yummy treats to enjoy afterwards as well!"

The young Imams (a) eyes shone with excitement as they all headed to the masjid for the evening salaah.

Later that night, after the young Imams (a) fell asleep, Sayyidah Fatimah (a) and Imam Ali (a) were tidying up the house. There was a knock on the door. Imam Ali (a) went to open it, finding a strange, tall and handsome man at the door.

"Salaamun alaikum O Imam Ali (a)!" greeted the man.

"Wa alaikum salaam, may I help you?" replied Imam Ali (a).

"I have come to deliver this package for our divine leaders of paradise. May Allah bless you and your family. Wasalaam!"

"JazakAllah, thank you. May Allah's blessings be on you as well!" replied Imam Ali (a).

Imam Ali (a) gave Sayyidah Fatimah (a) the package that the man had given. She opened it, finding two beautiful outfits and two pairs of shoes. "These must be from your father, the Prophet (s) of Allah! I didn't ask the tailor to sew any clothes!" Imam Ali (a) explained to Sayyidah Fatimah (a). "Alhamdulillah" she said smiling, happy that her two young sons had received new clothes for Eid!

It was the day of Eid! The two young Imams (a) woke up with a smile on their faces, excited for Eid. They ran to find their parents to hug them. However, before they could find them, they saw two sets of new clothes.

"Hasan (a)! Are these our new Eid clothes?" asked Imam Husain (a).

Before Imam Hasan (a) could respond, they heard Sayyidah Fatimah's (a) voice behind them. "Salaamun alaikum my two beloved sons. Eid Mubarak! Yes! These are your new Eid clothes!" "Wa alaikum salam and Eid Mubarak Mama!" The two Imams (a) replied kissing their mother's hand and giving her a huge hug.

The brothers did their Eid ghusl and wore their new clothes. When they finished getting ready, they were pleasantly surprised to see their beloved grandfather, Rasulullah (s), talking to their parents.

"Salaamun alaikum grandfather! Eid Mubarak!" the two young Imams (a) said enthusiastically and ran to give him a hug.

"Wa alaikum salaam my dear children! Eid Mubarak my little leaders from heaven! MashaAllah, look at your beautiful clothes!" exclaimed Rasulullah (a). He turned to Sayyidah Fatimah (a) and Imam Ali (a) and asked, "Do you know who sent these clothes for your blessed sons?"

Sayyidah Fatimah's (a) eyes grew wide in surprise. "O father, didn't you send these clothes for Hasan (a) and Husain (a)?" she asked.

"No, I didn't, my dear daughter. Someone Great has sent this gift! The man who came to deliver the package was an angel named Ridwan. He visited me after he delivered the package and told me that Allah the Almighty had sent these clothes for His appointed divine guides, the two young Imams (a), Hasan (a) and Husain (a). Because you placed your trust in Allah alone, and you and your family give for His sake alone, Allah has graced you with a gift from the heavens!"

Sayyidah Fatimah (a) broke into a smile and immediately thanked Allah for such a divine honor. Happiness filled her heart as they walked toward the masjid, their clothes shining under the bright morning sun!

Biḥār ul Anwār, Vol.43, Pg. 289, Hadith #52

Glossary

(a) - An abbreviation for the Arabic term ʿalayhi salaam, which means "Peace be upon him"

(s) - An abbreviation for the Arabic term salallahu ʿalayhi wa aalihi wa salam, which means "May God's peace and blessings be upon him and his family"

Al-Ghafoor - A title of God, meaning the All-Forgiving

Alhamdulillah - All praise is for God

Allah - The Arabic term for God, a culmination of all His holy names and titles

Ar-Raziq - A title of God, meaning the Provider (of sustenance)

Az-Zahra - The radiant one; a title of Sayyidah Fatimah (a), the daughter of the Prophet Muhammad (s)

Bazaar - A market in a Middle Eastern country

Dhuhr - The midday prayer performed daily by the Muslims, consisting of four units

Dua - Supplication: a confidential prayer between an individual and God

Eid - A Muslim holiday or celebration

Eid Mubarak - A greeting exchanged on the day of Eid, meaning "Have a blessed Eid"

Ghusl - Purifying oneself by washing the entire body from head to toe

Iftaar - The evening meal by which the Muslims open their fasts

Imam - A leader

Imam Ali (a) - The first Shi'a Imam or leader

Imam Hasan (a) - The second Shi'a Imam or leader; the eldest grandson of the Prophet Muhammad (s)

Imam Husain (a)- The third Shi'a Imam or leader; the second eldest grandson of the Prophet Muhammad (s)

InshaAllah - God-willing

Jamaal - Beauty

JazakAllah - An expression of gratitude, meaning "May Allah reward you"

Jibraeel - The Archangel Gabriel

Lady of Light - A title of Sayyidah Fatimah (a), the daughter of the Prophet Muhammad (s)

MashaAllah - That which Allah wishes; used as an expression of praise

Masjid - Mosque: a Muslim place of worship

Quran - The Holy Book of Islam

Ramadhan - The ninth lunar month in the Islamic calendar, which is also the month of fasting

Rasulullah (s) - The Messenger of God, a term used for Prophet Muhammad (s)

Sajdah - Prostration: the act of bringing the head to the ground; the utmost action of submission in Islam

Salaah - The daily prayer

Salaamun Alaikum - An Arabic greeting that means "Peace be upon you"

Sayyidah - Leader or chief (female)

Shifa'ah - Intercession: asking or approaching God through another person

SubhanAllah - All glory is for Allah (God)

Umm - Mother (of)

Wa Alaikum Salaam - A reply to the greeting Salaamun Alaikum, which means, "And peace be upon you"

Wahi - Divine revelation from God

Wudhu - Ablution: a sequential act of purifying oneself with water

Ya Rabbi - An expression meaning "O my Lord!"